COLOR THRU HISTORY

The People of the Ancient World
Elementary Supplement

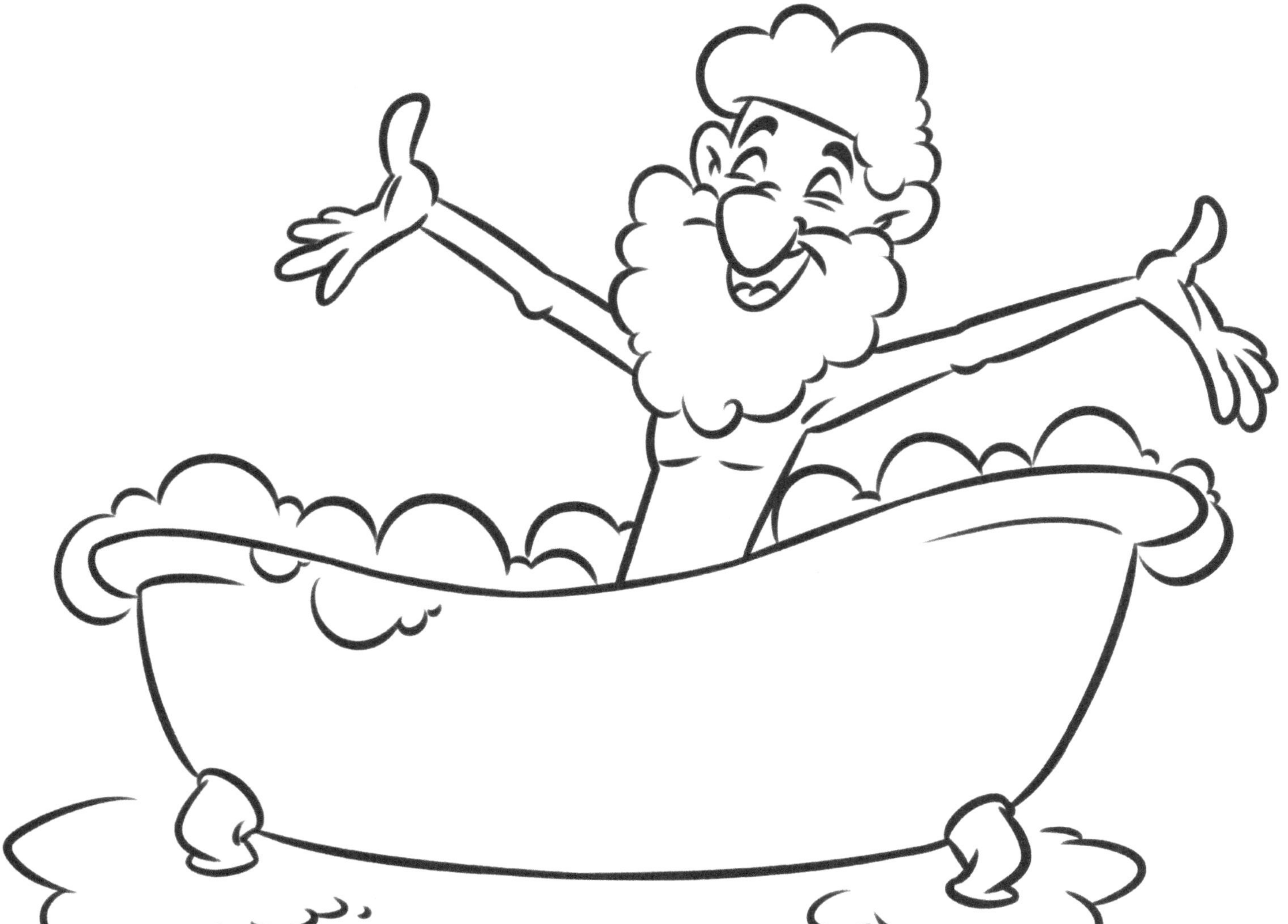

Fulton, KY

Current and upcoming titles:

Learn and Color Nature Series
- Medicinal Herbs
- Freshwater Fish
- Garden Edibles
- Reptiles

Learn and Color Stained Glass Series
- Landscapes & Seascapes
- Fish & Fowl
- Flowers

- Early Civilization
- The Ancient World
- The Middle Ages
- The Renaissance and Reformation
- The Industrial Revolution
- The Modern Age
- The Computer Age

Color Thru History™ – *The People of the Ancient World Elementary Supplement*
© 2020 Master Design Marketing, LLC

All rights reserved. This book or parts thereof may not be reproduced in any form, stored in any retrieval system, or transmitted in any form by any means—electronic, mechanical, photocopy, recording, or otherwise—without prior written permission of the publisher, except as provided by United States of America copyright law or as noted below. For permission requests, write to the publisher, at "Permissions Coordinator," at the address below.

Learn & Color Books
 an imprint of Master Design Marketing, LLC
 789 State Route 94 E
 Fulton, KY 42041
 www.LearnAndColor.com

Permission is granted to make as many photocopies as you need for your own immediate family's homeschool use. All other use is strictly prohibited. Co-ops and schools may NOT photocopy any portion of this book. Educators must purchase one book for each student.

For information about special discounts available for bulk purchases, sales promotions, fund-raising and educational needs, contact Learn & Color Books at sales@LearnAndColor.com.

ISBN: 978-1-947482-25-8
Cover and interior design by Faithe F Thomas
Research by Caitlyn F Williams
Some images are © Faithe F Thomas
All other Images © DepositPhotos.com
Text in this book is a derivative of information by Wikipedia.com, used under CC BY 4.0.
The text of this book is licensed under CC BY 4.0 by Faithe F Thomas.
Look for the Scottish Flag somewhere in each of our books.

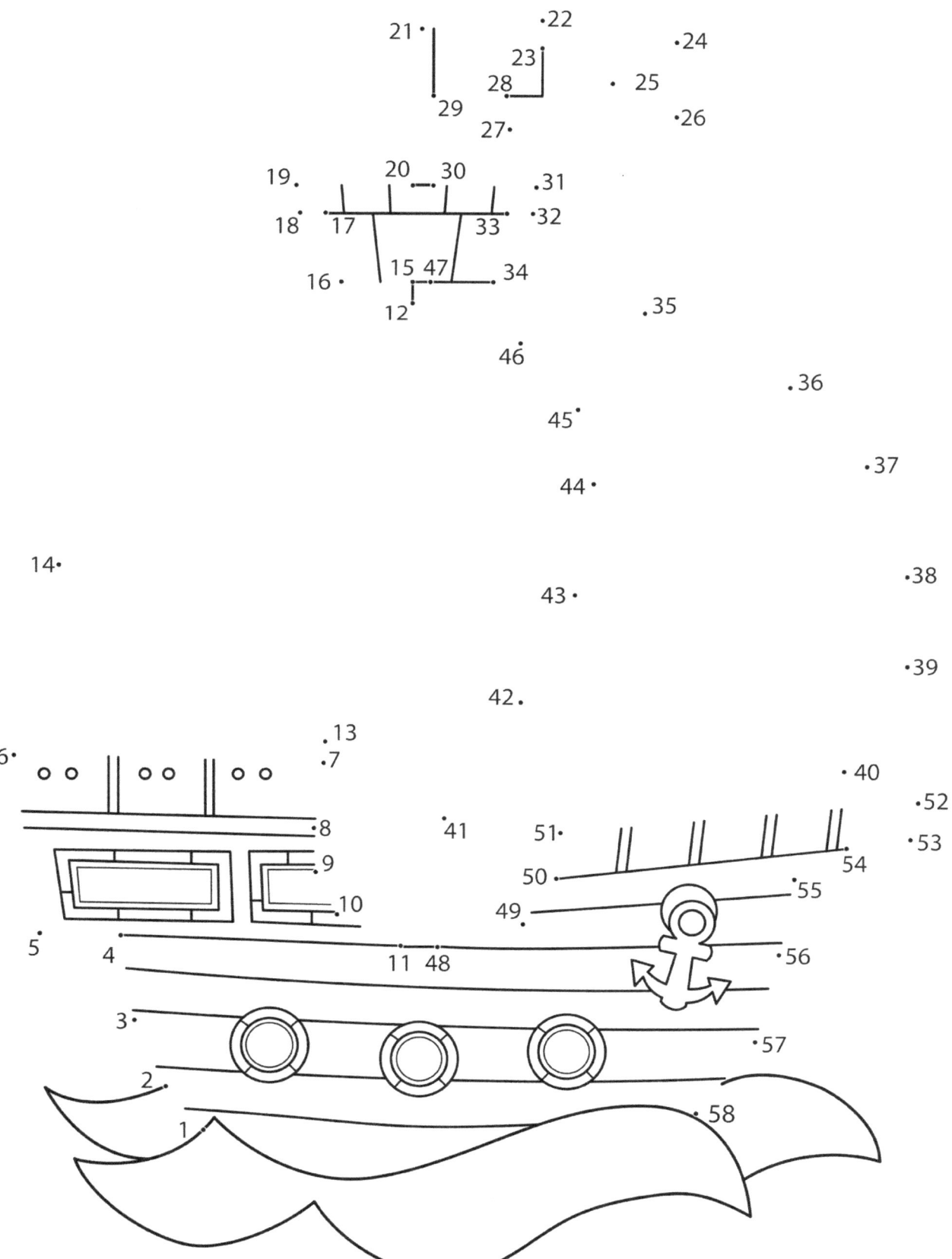

Herodotus was an ancient Greek historian who was the "father of history." He travelled around most of the known world, recording history.

Socrates was known for the pursuit of knowledge.
He taught famous people like Plato and Xenophon.

Thucydides was an Athenian historian and general.
He wrote about the war between Sparta and Athens.
Thucydides has been called the father of "scientific history."

Hippocrates of Kos is known as the "father of medicine." He is known for coining the Hippocratic Oath, which is the oath that doctors and medical students take before their practice.

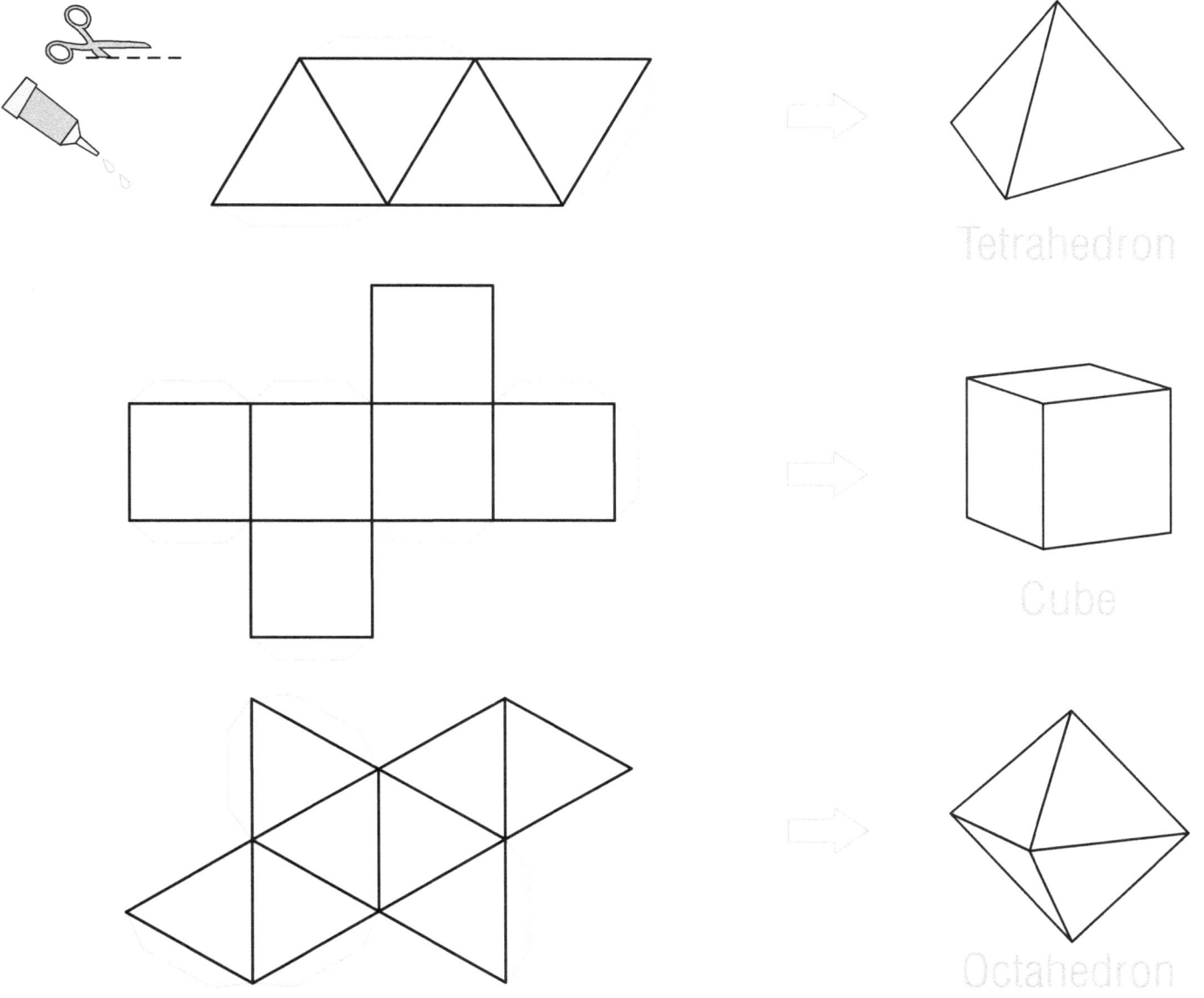

Plato was a philosopher in classical Greece and the founder of the Academy in Athens, the first institution of higher learning in the Western world.

Aristotle was one of the most important Western philosophers. He was a student of Plato and the teacher of Alexander the Great.

Alexander the Great was the King of Macedon. He created one of the largest empires of the ancient world, stretching from Greece to northwestern India. He is one of history's most successful military commanders.

Euclid of Alexandria was the father of geometry.
He wrote the main textbook for teaching math (especially geometry)
used from the time of its publication until the early 20th century.

Ashoka was an Indian emperor of the Maurya Dynasty.
He is remembered for the Ashoka pillars.

EUREKA!!

Archimedes of Syracuse was a Greek who loved math. He reportedly proclaimed "Eureka! Eureka!" after he had stepped into a bath and noticed that the water level rose.

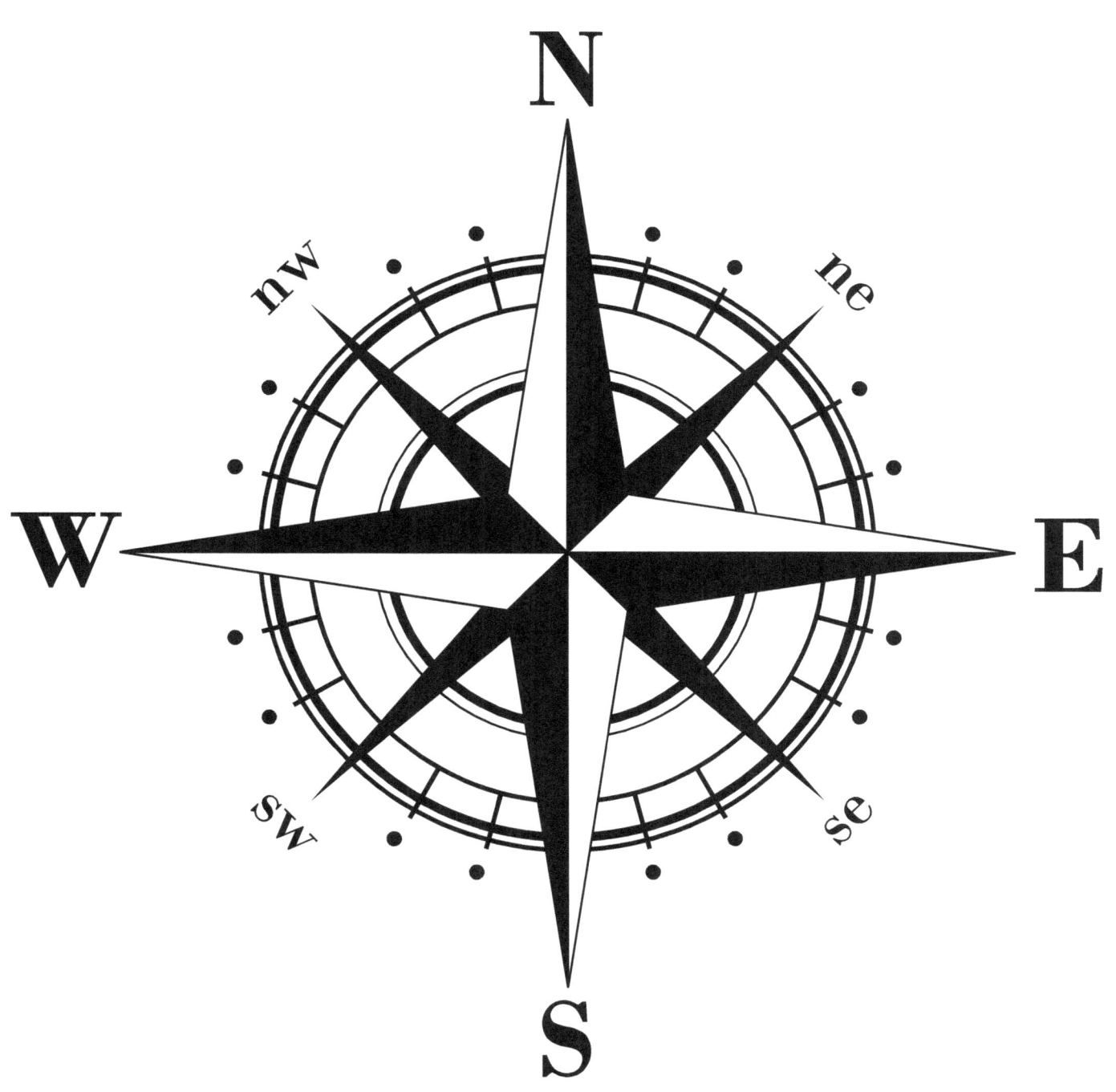

Eratosthenes of Cyrene loved math and geography.
He invented the study of geography,
including the terminology used today.

Qin Shi Huang, also known as King Ying Zheng,
unified the warring states of China and became the First Emperor.
He created the Great Wall of China.

Hannibal Barca was a Carthaginian general.
His army included war elephants.

Spartacus was a Thracian gladiator
who escaped slave leaders to lead a revolt.

Marcus Tullius Cicero was a Roman statesman, lawyer, and philosopher. He was best known for his speeches.

Gaius Julius Caesar was a Roman politician and military general.
He created our current calendar.

Virgil was an ancient Roman poet. He wrote the epic *Aeneid*.
It follows the Trojan refugee Aeneas as he struggles
to fulfill his destiny and reach Italy.

Cleopatra was a ruler of Egypt.
She was a diplomat, naval commander, linguist, and medical author.

Augustus Caius Julius Caesar Octavianus was the first Emperor of the Roman Empire. He was ruler when Jesus was born. The month of August is named after Augustus.

Ovid was a Roman poet.
He is best known for a book called *Metamorphoses*.

Jesus was a Jewish preacher and religious leader. Christians believe he is God the Son and the Messiah (Christ) prophesied in the ancient Hebrew Scriptures.

Seneca the Younger was a Roman philosopher.
He was a tutor and later advisor to Emperor Nero.

Paul the Apostle, also known as Saul of Tarsus,
wrote 13 books of the New Testament.
He was shipwrecked three times!

Boudica was a queen of the British Celtic Iceni tribe.
She nearly drove the Romans out of the British Isles.
But Nero's army won.

Nero Claudius Caesar Augustus Germanicus was ruler of the Roman Empire. He burned parts of Rome to make room for his large palace. He blamed Christians for the fire.

Galen of Pergamon was the personal physician to several Roman emperors. His theories dominated and influenced Western medical science for more than 1,300 years.

Constantine the Great was ruler of the Roman Empire.
He moved the capital to Constantinople (now Istanbul).
He was the first Roman emperor to convert to Christianity.

Augustine of Hippo was a Roman African, early Christian theologian, and philosopher from Numidia (Algeria). His writings influenced Western Christianity and Western philosophy.

Attila the Hun was one of the most feared enemies of the Roman Empire. He was called the *Scourge of God* by the Romans.

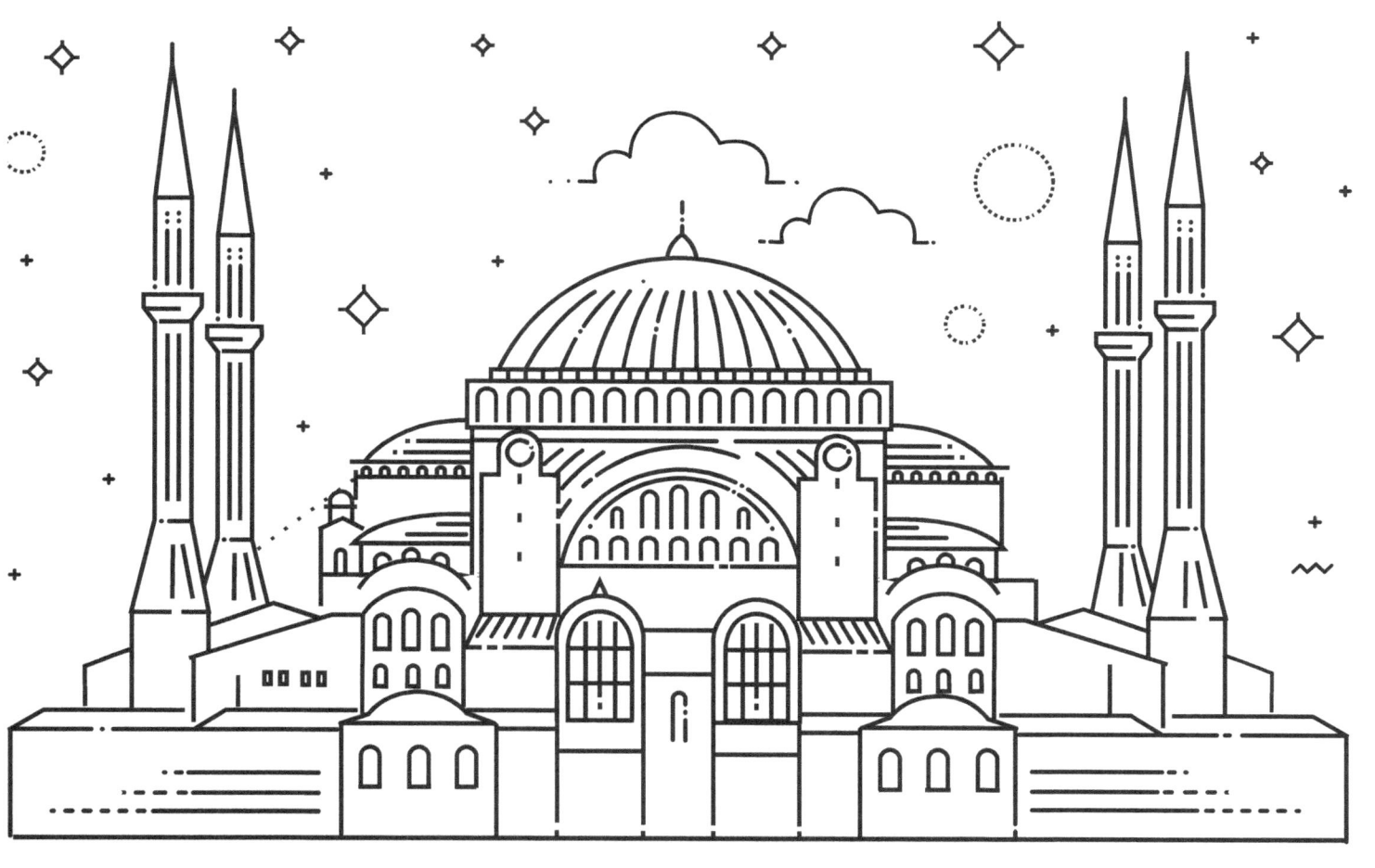

Justinian the Great was an Eastern Roman emperor.
He built the church of Hagia Sophia in Istanbul.

www.ingramcontent.com/pod-product-compliance
Lightning Source LLC
Chambersburg PA
CBHW081756100526
44592CB00015B/2461